100 facts on
Ancient Egypt

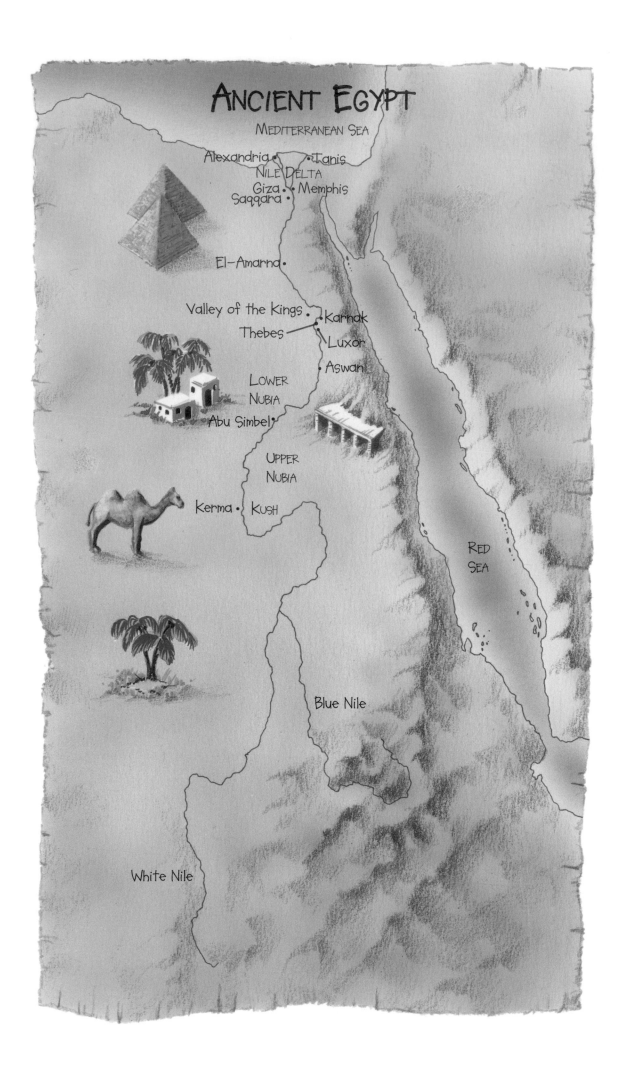

ANCIENT EGYPT

MEDITERRANEAN SEA

Alexandria • • Tanis
NILE DELTA
Giza • • Memphis
Saqqara •

El-Amarna •

Valley of the Kings •
Thebes ⸺ • Karnak
• Luxor
• Aswan

LOWER
NUBIA

Abu Simbel •

UPPER
NUBIA

Kerma • KUSH

RED
SEA

Blue Nile

White Nile

100 facts on

Ancient Egypt

Jane Walker

Consultant: Richard Tames

Miles
KELLY
PUBLISHING

First published as hardback in 2001 by Miles Kelly Publishing Ltd
Bardfield Centre, Great Bardfield, Essex, CM7 4SL

This edition published in 2008

4 6 8 10 9 7 5 3

Editorial Director: Belinda Gallagher
Art Director: Jo Brewer
Editorial Assistant: Bethanie Bourne
Volume Designer: Sally Lace
Picture Researcher: Liberty Newton
Proofreader/Indexer: Lynn Bresler
Production Manager: Elizabeth Brunwin
Reprographics: Anthony Cambray, Mike Coupe, Ian Paulyn

ISBN 978-1-84236-759-9

Printed in China

British Library Cataloguing-in-Publication Data
A catalogue record for this book is available from the British Library

ACKNOWLEDGEMENTS
The publishers would like to thank the following artists
who have contributed to this book:
Chris Buzer/Studio Galante, Vanessa Card, Mike Foster/Maltings Partnership,
Terry Gabbey/AFA, Peter Gregory, Richard Hook/Linden Artists Ltd,
John James/Temple Rogers, Janos Marffy, Roger Payne/Linden Artists Ltd,
Eric Rowe/Linden Artists Ltd, Peter Sarson, Rob Sheffield
Nick Spender/Advocate, Roger Stewart, Rudi Vizi
Mike White/Temple Rogers

Cartoons by Mark Davis at Mackerel

All other images come from MKP Archives

www.mileskelly.net
info@mileskelly.net

www.factsforprojects.com

Contents

Heart of ancient Egypt 6

Royal news 8

Powerful people 10

Magnificent monuments 12

Supreme beings 14

In tombs and temples 16

Big building blocks 18

Making mummies 20

War and enemies 22

Bartering and buying 24

The farmer's year 26

Getting around 28

Who's who 30

Home sweet home 32

Dressing up 34

Baking and brewing 36

Hard day's work 38

Clever Egyptians 40

From pictures to words 42

Fun and games 44

Heroes and heroines 46

Index 48

The heart of ancient Egypt

1 **Without the waters of the river Nile, the amazing civilization of ancient Egypt might never have existed.** The Nile provided water for drinking and for watering crops. Every year its floods left a strip of rich dark soil on both sides of the river. Farmers grew their crops in these fertile strips. The Egyptians called their country Kemet, which means 'black land', after this dark soil. The Nile was also important for transport, it was a motorway for the Egyptians!

Royal news

2 **The rulers of ancient Egypt were called pharaohs.** The word 'pharaoh' means great house. The pharaoh was the most important and powerful person in the country. Many people believed he was a god.

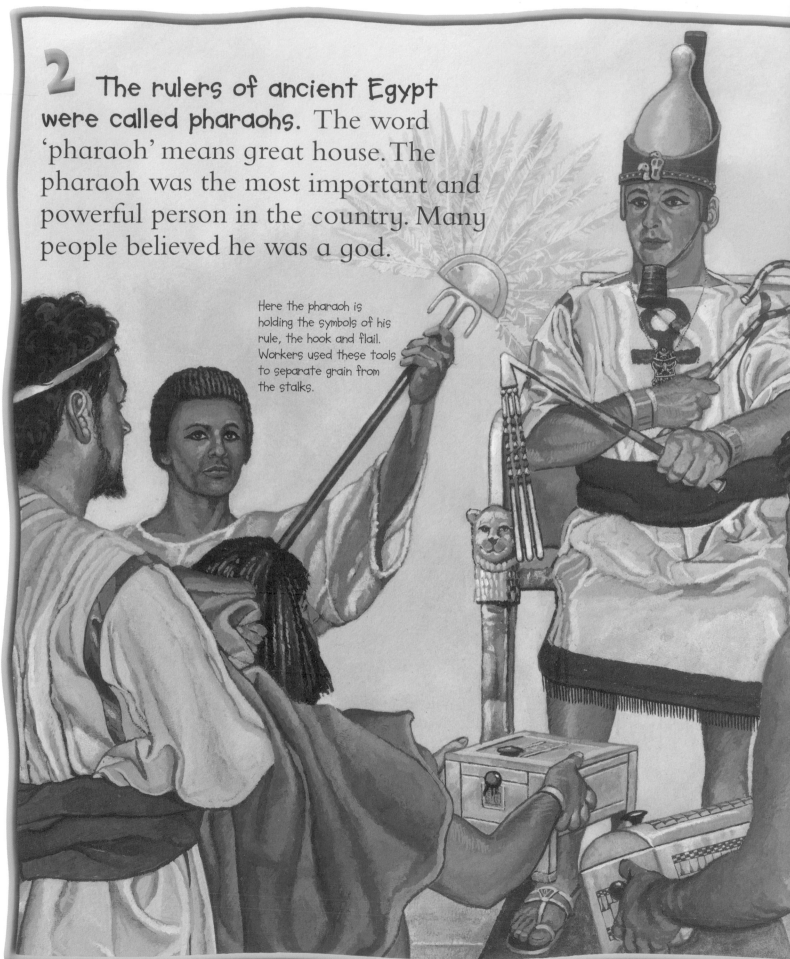

Here the pharaoh is holding the symbols of his rule, the hook and flail. Workers used these tools to separate grain from the stalks.

3 **Ramses II ruled for over 60 years.** He was the only pharaoh to carry the title 'the Great' after his name. Ramses was a great builder and a brave soldier. He was also the father of an incredibly large number of children: 96 boys and 60 girls. Just imagine having 156 brothers and sisters!

These people are paying tribute to the pharaoh. This means that they have come from the surrounding countries to give him presents and tell him how great he is!

4 **The pharaoh often married a close female relative, such as his sister or half-sister.** In this way the blood of the royal family remained pure. The title of 'pharaoh' was usually passed on to the eldest son of the pharaoh's most important wife.

I DON'T BELIEVE IT!

On special occasions, women courtiers wore hair cones made of animal fat scented with spices and herbs. The melting fat trickled down their heads, making their hair sweet smelling – and greasy!

Powerful people

5 Over 30 different dynasties ruled ancient Egypt. A dynasty is a line of rulers from the same family.

6 More than 7,000 years ago, people from central Africa began to arrive in Egypt. They settled in villages along the banks of the Nile and around the Nile Delta. These villages formed the two kingdoms of Upper Egypt (Nile Valley) and Lower Egypt (Nile Delta).

Crown of Lower Egypt

Crown of Upper Egypt

▲ The double crown of Egypt was made up of two crowns, the bucket-shaped red crown of Lower Egypt and the bottle-shaped white crown of Upper Egypt.

▼ This timeline shows the dates of the dynasties of ancient Egypt. The dates are given as a year BC. This means Before Christ. We also say AD, by which we mean After Christ. The year 1 AD is the date from which we start counting the years.

Egypt's first pyramid, the Step Pyramid, was built in 2650 BC.

2750–2250 BC
OLD KINGDOM
(Dynasties III–VI)

The Hyksos people invaded in 1670 BC and introduced the chariot.

2025–1627 BC
MIDDLE KINGDOM
(Dynasties XI–XIII)

The tomb of the New Kingdom pharaoh Tutankhamun was discovered in 1922.

1539–1070 BC
NEW KINGDOM
(Dynasties XVIII–XX)

3100–2750 BC
EARLY DYNASTIC PERIOD
(Dynasties I and II)

King Narmer, also called Menes, unites Egypt and records his deeds on what we call the Narmer palette.

2250–2025 BC
FIRST INTERMEDIATE PERIOD
(Dynasties VII–X)

As the civilization of Egypt progressed they introduced gods for all different areas of life.

1648–1539 BC
SECOND INTERMEDIATE PERIOD
(Dynasties XIV–XVII)

Nilometers were invented to keep track of the height of the river which was very important for the crops.

1070–653 BC
THIRD INTERMEDIATE PERIOD
(Dynasties XXI–XXV)

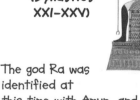

The god Ra was identified at this time with Amun, and became Amun–Ra who was the king of the gods.

7 The history of ancient Egypt began more than 5,000 years ago. The first period was called the Old Kingdom, when the Egyptians built the Great Pyramids. Next came the Middle Kingdom and finally the New Kingdom.

◀ Pharaoh Pepi II (2246–2152 BC), had the longest reign in history – 94 years. He became king when he was only 6 years old.

Queen Cleopatra was the last ruler of the Ptolemaic period.

**332–30 BC
PTOLEMAIC PERIOD**

**664–332 BC
LATE PERIOD
(Dynasties
XXVI–XXXI)**

In 332 BC Alexander the Great conquered Egypt and founded the famous city of Alexandria.

**30 BC–AD 395
ROMAN PERIOD**

The Roman Emperor Octavian conquered Egypt in 30 BC.

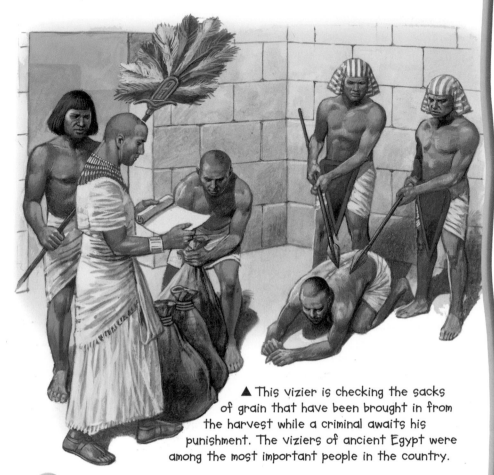

▲ This vizier is checking the sacks of grain that have been brought in from the harvest while a criminal awaits his punishment. The viziers of ancient Egypt were among the most important people in the country.

8 Officials called viziers helped the pharaoh to govern Egypt. Each ruler appointed two viziers – one each for Upper and Lower Egypt. Viziers were powerful men. Each vizier was in charge of a number of royal overseers. Each overseer was responsible for a particular area of government, for example the army or granaries where the grain was stored. The pharaoh, though, was in charge of everyone.

I DON'T BELIEVE IT!

Farmers tried to bribe tax collectors by offering them gifts of goats or ducks in exchange for a smaller tax charge.

Magnificent monuments

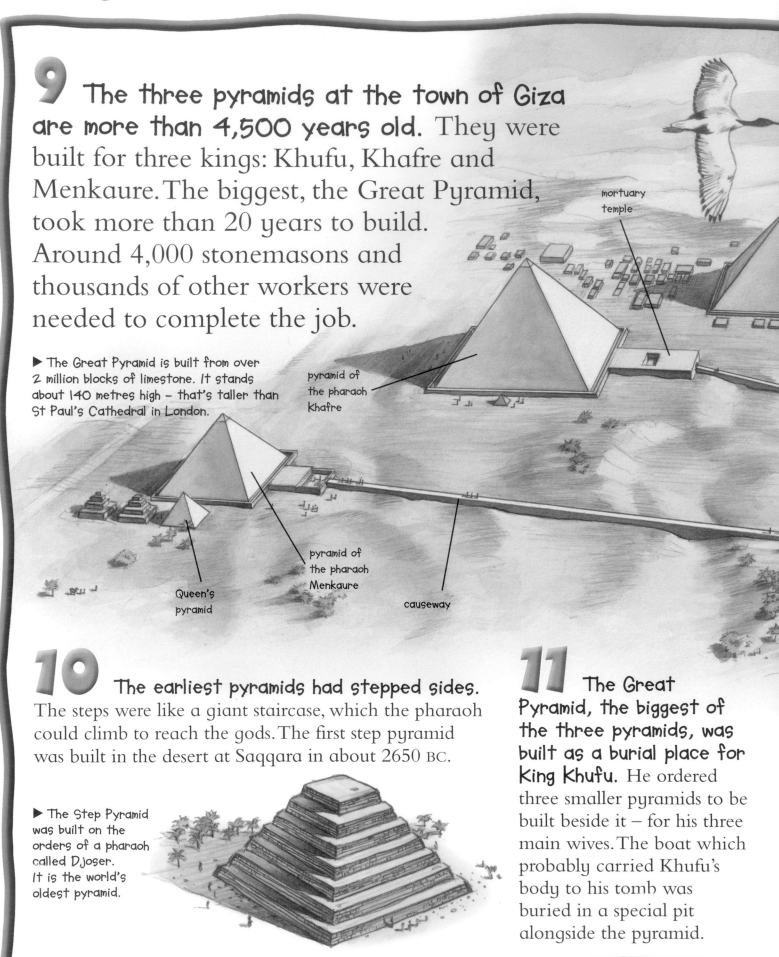

9 The three pyramids at the town of Giza are more than 4,500 years old. They were built for three kings: Khufu, Khafre and Menkaure. The biggest, the Great Pyramid, took more than 20 years to build. Around 4,000 stonemasons and thousands of other workers were needed to complete the job.

▶ The Great Pyramid is built from over 2 million blocks of limestone. It stands about 140 metres high – that's taller than St Paul's Cathedral in London.

mortuary temple

pyramid of the pharaoh Khafre

pyramid of the pharaoh Menkaure

Queen's pyramid

causeway

10 The earliest pyramids had stepped sides. The steps were like a giant staircase, which the pharaoh could climb to reach the gods. The first step pyramid was built in the desert at Saqqara in about 2650 BC.

▶ The Step Pyramid was built on the orders of a pharaoh called Djoser. It is the world's oldest pyramid.

11 The Great Pyramid, the biggest of the three pyramids, was built as a burial place for King Khufu. He ordered three smaller pyramids to be built beside it – for his three main wives. The boat which probably carried Khufu's body to his tomb was buried in a special pit alongside the pyramid.

the Great Pyramid of the pharaoh Khufu

Queen's pyramid

stone mastaba tombs for royal family and courtiers

sphinx guarding the pyramid

valley temple

Underground chamber

Pharaoh's Chamber

Grand Gallery

Queen's Chamber

Boat pit

12 The Great Sphinx at Giza guards the way to the Great Pyramid. It is a huge stone statue with the body of a lion and the head of a human. The features on the face were carved to look like the pharaoh Khafre.

I DON'T BELIEVE IT!

A special handbook for tomb robbers called 'The Book of Buried Pearls' gave details of hidden treasures and tips for sneaking past the spirits that guarded the dead!

13 Tomb robbers broke into the pyramids to steal the fabulous treasures inside. To make things difficult for the robbers, pyramid builders added heavy doors of granite and built false corridors inside the pyramids.

14 Inside the Great Pyramid were two large burial rooms, one each for the pharaoh and queen. The Pharaoh's Chamber was reached by a corridor called the Grand Gallery, with a roof more than 8 metres above the floor, four times higher than a normal ceiling. Once the king's body was inside the burial chamber, the entrance was sealed with stone blocks. The last workers had to leave by specially built escape passages.

Supreme beings

15 The ancient Egyptians worshipped more than 1,000 different gods and goddesses. The most important god of all was Ra, the sun god. People believed that he was swallowed up each evening by the sky goddess Nut. During the night Ra travelled through the underworld and was born again each morning.

◄ The sun god Ra later became Amun-Ra. He was combined with another god to make a new king of the gods.

16 A god was often shown as an animal, or as half-human, half-animal. Below are some of the well-known gods that were represented by animals. Sobek was a god of the river Nile. Crocodiles were kept in pools next to Sobek's temples. Bastet was the goddess of cats, musicians and dancers. The cat was a sacred animal in ancient Egypt. When a pet cat died, the body would be wrapped and laid in a cat-shaped coffin before burial in the city's cat cemetery. The moon god Thoth usually had the head of an ibis, but he was sometimes shown as a baboon. The ancient Egyptians believed that hieroglyphic writing came from Thoth.

Bastet

Sobek

Thoth

17 As god of the dead, Osiris was in charge of the underworld. Ancient Egyptians believed that dead people travelled to the kingdom of the underworld below the Earth. Osiris and his wife Isis were the parents of the god Horus, protector of the pharaoh.

Isis

Osiris

Horus

18 Anubis was in charge of preparing bodies to be mummified. This work was known as embalming. Because jackals were often found near cemeteries, Anubis, who watched over the dead, was given the form of a jackal. Egyptian priests often wore Anubis masks when preparing mummies.

Anubis

QUIZ 1

1. Who was buried inside the Great Pyramid?

2. Describe the crown of Upper Egypt.

3. What was a vizier?

4. Which pharaoh ruled for over 90 years?

5. What is the Great Sphinx?

1. King Khufu 2. A bottle-shaped white crown 3. An important governor 4. Pepi II 5. An animal with the body of a lion and the head of a human

19 A pharaoh called Amenhotep IV changed his name to Akhenaten, after the sun god Aten. During his reign Akhenaten worshipped only Aten and made Aten the king of all the gods.

In tombs and temples

20 From about 2150 BC pharaohs were not buried in pyramids, but in tombs in the Valley of the Kings. At that time it was a fairly remote place, surrounded by steep cliffs lying on the west bank of the Nile opposite the city of Thebes. Some of the tombs were cut into the cliffside, others were built deep underground.

▲ Robbers looted everything from the royal tombs – gold, silver, precious stones, furniture, clothing, pots – sometimes they even stole the dead ruler's body!

21 Like the pyramids, the riches in the royal tombs attracted robbers. The entrance to the Valley of the Kings was guarded, but robbers had broken into every tomb except one within 1,000 years. The only one they missed was the tomb of the boy king Tutankhamun, and even this had been partially robbed and re-sealed.

▲ The solid gold death mask of Tutankhamun found in the Valley of the Kings. The young king's tomb was discovered, with its contents untouched, about 80 years ago.

annexe

statues of the king

antechamber

tomb entrance

22 Archaeologist Howard Carter discovered the tomb of Tutankhamun in 1922. An archaeologist is someone who searches for historical objects. Tutankhamun's body was found inside a nest of three mummy cases in a sarcophagus (stone coffin). The sarcophagus was inside a set of four wooden shrines big enough to contain a modern car.

decorated shrines, with the coffins and sarcophagus

decorated walls of the burial chamber

Anubis, the jackal-headed god

golden shrine containing the canopic jars

treasure room

Carter, and his sponsor Lord Carnarvon, finally found Tutankhamun's tomb after five years of archaeological exploration in Egypt. Carnarvon died just 4 months after he first entered the tomb. Some people said he was the victim of Tutankhamun's 'curse' because he had disturbed the pharaoh's body. In fact Carnarvon died from an infected mosquito bite.

23 The ancient Egyptians built fabulous temples to worship their gods. Powerful priests ruled over the temples, and the riches and lands attached to them. Many of the finest temples were dedicated to Amun-Ra, king of the gods.

24 The temple at Abu Simbel, in the south of Egypt, is carved out of sandstone rock. It was built on the orders of Ramses II. The temple was built in such a way that on two days each year (February 22 and October 22) the Sun's first rays shine on the back of the inner room, lighting up statues of the gods.

▲ Four enormous statues of Ramses II, each over 20 metres high, guard the temple entrance at Abu Simbel.

Big building blocks!

25 Each block used to build the Great Pyramid weighed as much as two and a half adult elephants! Labourers used copper chisels and saws to cut and shape the stones before dragging them on wooden sledges to the base of the pyramid.

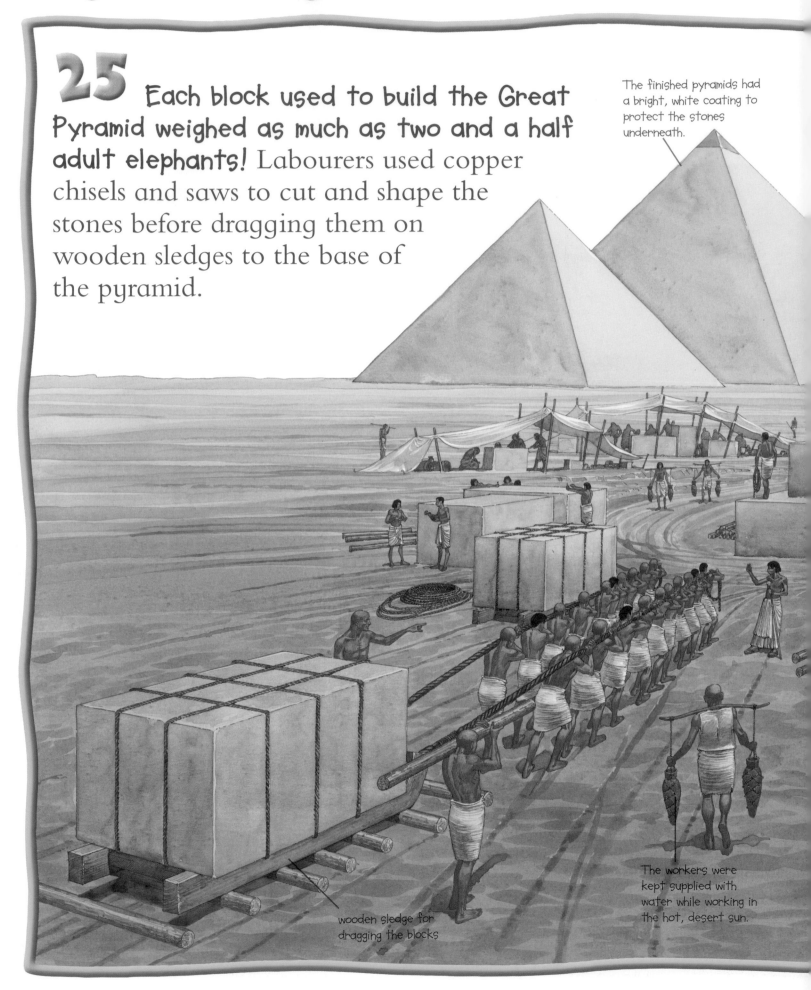

The finished pyramids had a bright, white coating to protect the stones underneath.

wooden sledge for dragging the blocks

The workers were kept supplied with water while working in the hot, desert sun.

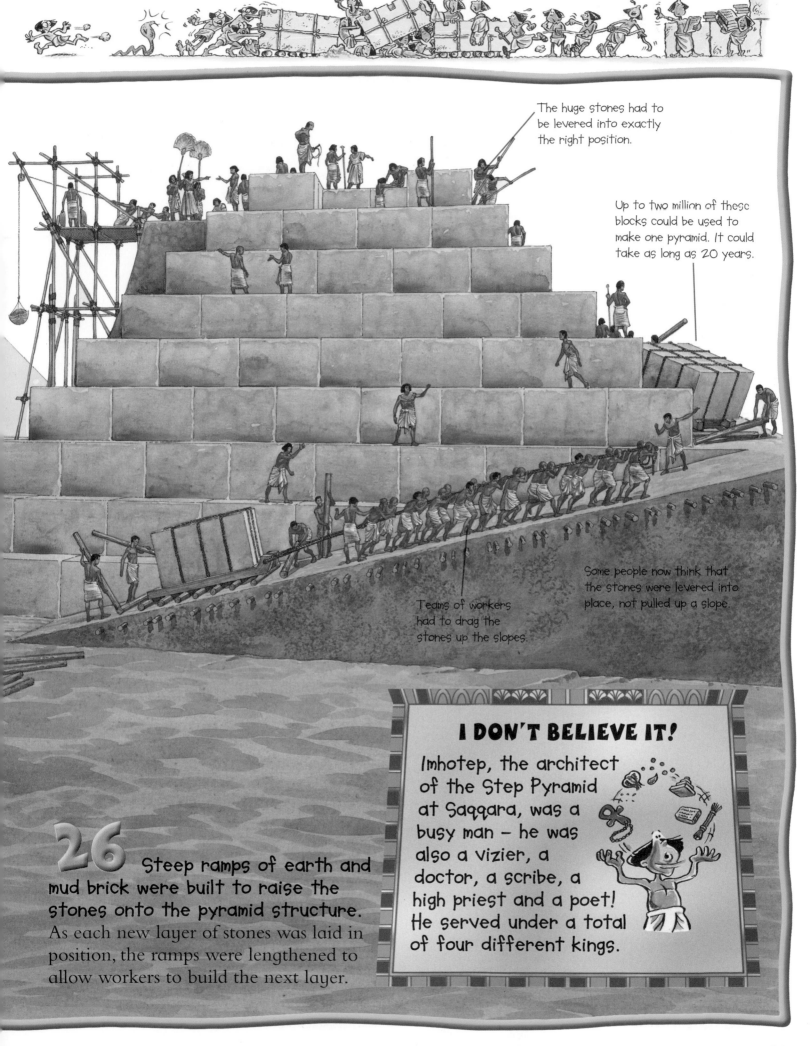

The huge stones had to be levered into exactly the right position.

Up to two million of these blocks could be used to make one pyramid. It could take as long as 20 years.

Teams of workers had to drag the stones up the slopes.

Some people now think that the stones were levered into place, not pulled up a slope.

26 Steep ramps of earth and mud brick were built to raise the stones onto the pyramid structure. As each new layer of stones was laid in position, the ramps were lengthened to allow workers to build the next layer.

I DON'T BELIEVE IT!

Imhotep, the architect of the Step Pyramid at Saqqara, was a busy man – he was also a vizier, a doctor, a scribe, a high priest and a poet! He served under a total of four different kings.

Making mummies

27 Making a mummy was difficult and skilled work. First the brain, stomach, lungs and other organs were removed, but the heart was left in place. Next, the body was covered with salts and left to dry for up to 40 days. The dried body was washed and filled with linen and other stuffing to keep its shape. Finally, it was oiled and wrapped in layers of linen bandages.

The priest in charge wore a jackal mask to represent the god Anubis.

mummified dog

mummified cat

The organs were stored in canopic jars like these. Each jar represented a god.

amulet placed with the mummy for luck

28 Animals were made into mummies too. A nobleman might be buried with a mummy of his pet cat. Mummification was expensive, so people only preserved animals in this way to offer them to the gods. One mummified crocodile discovered by archaeologists was over 4.5 metres long!

29 Body parts were removed from the dead person and stored in special containers. The stomach, intestines, lungs and liver were cut out and stored in four separate jars, called canopic jars.

wooden coffin
for the body

MAKE A DEATH MASK

You will need

a play mask (made of plastic or stiff card)
PVA glue   a paintbrush
newspaper   poster paints
white paint

Use an inexpensive play mask, such as a Halloween one, as your basic mask. Cover the mask with a thick layer of PVA glue. Spread layers of torn newspaper strips over the mask and leave to dry.

Cover the mask with white paint. When dry, use the poster paints to create an amazing death mask of your own! If you haven't got gold-coloured paint, you can use gold glitter to create the same effect.

30 **A mask was fitted over the face of a mummy.** The ancient Egyptians believed that the mask would help the dead person's spirit to recognize the mummy later on. A pharaoh's mummy mask was made of gold and precious stones.

31 **When ready for burial, a mummy was placed inside a special case.** Some cases were simple wooden boxes, but others were shaped like mummies and richly decorated. The mummy case of an important person, such as a pharaoh or a nobleman, was sealed inside a stone coffin called a sarcophagus.

War and enemies

32 Foot soldiers carried metal swords and spears, with shields made of wood or ox hide. Later, soldiers were protected by body armour made from strips of leather.

33 Specially trained soldiers fired arrows from their bows while riding in horse-drawn chariots. Each chariot carried two soldiers and was pulled by a pair of horses. During the time of the New Kingdom (around 3,500 years ago), this new kind of war weapon helped the Egyptians to defeat several invading armies.

▲ During the New Kingdom, Egypt created a professional army of trained soldiers. Soldiers had strong shields and a long and deadly spear.

▲ The Egyptians were gradually taken over by the Hyksos people from the east. The Hyksos introduced the horse-drawn chariot into Egypt. The Egyptians copied the chariot and eventually used it to defeat the Hyksos and drive them out.

34 **The Sea People attacked Egypt during the reign of Ramses III.** These raiders came from the northeastern corner of the Mediterranean. Ramses sent a fleet of warships to defeat them.

▼ Ramses III fought off three separate lots of invaders, including the Sea People. Warships were used by Ramses to defeat the Sea People.

steering oars

decorated prow

oars for power when there was no wind

▼ The Hyksos invaders conquered Lower Egypt during the 1700s BC. They did not reach Thebes, but made their capital at Avaris.

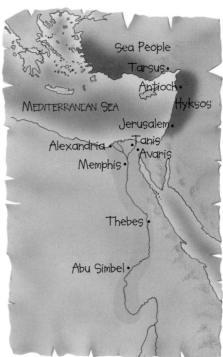

Sea People
Tarsus•
Antioch•
MEDITERRANEAN SEA   •Hyksos
Jerusalem•
Alexandria•   •Tanis
Memphis•   •Avaris

Thebes•

Abu Simbel•

35 **A general called Ptolemy won control of Egypt in 323 BC.** He was the first of several rulers who made up the Ptolemaic dynasty. Under the Ptolemies, the city of Alexandria, on the Mediterranean Sea, became the new Egyptian capital and an important city for art and culture.

fires kept burning to warn ships

▶ The great harbours at Alexandria were guarded by the huge Pharos, the first lighthouse in the world (and one of the Seven Wonders of the Ancient World). The city also had a museum and a vast library containing up to 500,000 books.

36 **The Hyksos people conquered Egypt in about 1700 BC.** They ruled the Egyptians for 200 years. They introduced the horse, the chariot and other new weapons which the Egyptians eventually used to conquer an empire.

I DON'T BELIEVE IT!
Soldiers who fought bravely in battle were awarded golden fly medals – for 'buzzing' the enemy so successfully!

Bartering and buying

37 Egyptian traders did not use money to buy and sell goods. Instead they bartered (exchanged goods) with other traders. Merchants visited the countries bordering the Mediterranean Sea as well as those lands to the south. The Egyptians offered goods such as gold, a kind of paper called papyrus, and cattle.

▲ These Egyptian workers are carrying their oil to market. When they arrive, they can exchange their oil for anything they need, such as food or clothes.

38 Merchants brought back exotic goods from the land of Nubia, to the south of Egypt. These included leopard skins, elephant tusks, ostrich feathers – and slaves. One of the main trading posts where goods were exchanged was the town of Kerma, on the river Nile beyond Egypt.

The gold mines in the deserts of eastern Egypt kept the country supplied with wealth. These mines helped make Egypt the richest country in the ancient world.

39 Egyptians traded with Syria, Lebanon, Cyprus and the Land of Israel (present-day Palestine) as well as with many African countries. Traders brought back silver from Syria, cedar wood, oils and horses from Lebanon, copper from Cyprus, a gem called lupis lazuli from Afghanistan, and ebony wood and ivory from central Africa.

I DON'T BELIEVE IT!

Fly swatters made from giraffe tails were a popular fashion item in ancient Egypt.

The Egyptians travelled to the land of Punt to bring back incense. We do not know exactly where the land of Punt is today, but we know that the Egyptians thought of it as a far away and exciting place.

40 When goods were sold they were weighed using a balance and special copper weights called deben. An item could be exchanged for its equivalent weight in copper. A bed, for example, had a value of 25 deben. Pieces of gold and silver were also weighed and used as payment.

The farmer's year

41 The farming year was divided into three seasons: the flood, the growing period and the harvest. Most people worked on the land, but farmers could not work between July and November because the land was covered by flood waters. Instead, they went off to help build the pyramids and royal palaces.

42 The river Nile used to flood its banks in July each year. The flood waters left a strip of rich black soil, about 10 km wide, along each bank. Apart from these fertile strips and a few scattered oases, pools of water in the desert, the rest of the land was mainly just sand.

44 Water was lifted from the Nile using a device called a shaduf. It was a long pole with a wooden bucket hanging from a rope at one end, and a weight at the other. The pole was supported by a wooden frame. One person working alone could operate a shaduf.

Tax collectors would often decide how rich a person was by counting how many cattle he owned.

43 Egyptian farmers had to water their crops because of the hot, dry climate with no rain. They dug special channels around their fields along which the waters of the Nile could flow. In this way farmers could water their crops all year round. This was called irrigation, and it is still done today.

Almost no rain fell on the dry, dusty farmland of ancient Egypt. No crops would grow properly without the water from the Nile.

45 Farmers used wooden ploughs pulled by oxen to prepare the soil for planting. They also had wooden hoes. The seeds were mainly planted by hand. At harvest time, wooden sickles edged with stone teeth were used to cut the crops.

46 Harvesting the grain was only the start of the process. In the threshing room people would beat the grain to separate it from the chaff, the shell, of the grain. It was then winnowed. Men would throw the grain and chaff up into the air and fan away the chaff. The heavier grain dropped straight to the floor. The grain was then gathered up and taken to the granary to be stored.

47 Wheat and barley (for bread and beer) were the two main crops grown by the ancient Egyptians. They also grew grapes (for wine) and flax (to make linen). A huge variety of fruits and vegetables grew in the fertile soil, including dates, figs, cucumbers, melons, onions, peas, leeks and lettuces.

I DON'T BELIEVE IT!

Instead of using scarecrows, Egyptian farmers hired young boys to scare away the birds – they had to have a loud voice and a good aim with a slingshot!

Farmers had to hand over part of their harvest each year as a tax payment. It was usually given to the local temple in exchange for use of the temple's land.

48 Egyptian farmers kept cattle as well as goats, sheep, ducks and geese. Some farmers kept bees to produce honey, which was used for sweetening cakes and other foods.

winnowers separate the grain from the chaff

Getting around

49 The main method of transport in ancient Egypt was by boat along the river Nile. The Nile is the world's longest river. It flows across the entire length of the desert lands of Egypt.

50 The earliest kinds of boat were made from papyrus reeds. They were propelled by a long pole and, later on, by oars. Gradually, wooden boats replaced the reed ones, and sails were added.

These early boats were made of bundles of reeds tied together.

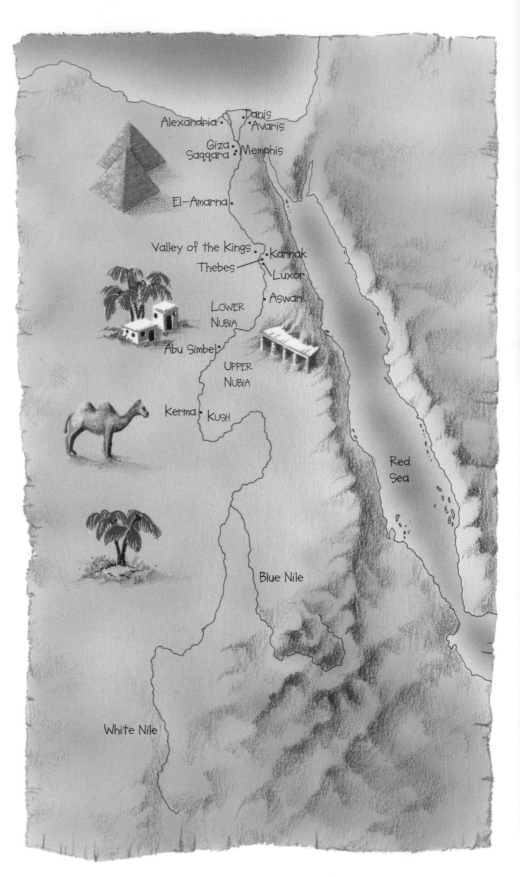

▲ The total length of the river Nile is around 6,670 kilometres. To the south of Egypt, the Nile has two main branches – the White Nile and the Blue Nile.

51 A magnificent carved boat was built to carry the body of King Khufu at his funeral. Over 43 metres long, it was built from planks of cedar wood. The boat was buried in a special pit next to the Great Pyramid.

▼ The cabin on board Khufu's funerary boat was decorated with carved flowers. Other traditional designs were carved into the boat. The joints were held together with strips of leather.

steering oars

cabin for coffin

52 Wooden barges carried blocks of limestone across the river Nile for the pyramids and temples. The stone came from quarries on the opposite bank to the site of the pyramids. The granite used to build the insides of the pyramids came from much farther away – from quarries at Aswan 800 kilometres upstream.

Simple wooden barges like these were essential for the building work that went on in Egypt.

QUIZ 2

How well do you know your gods and goddesses? Can you name these:

1. This god has a jackal's head and hangs around dead bodies.

2. This god's magic eye will protect you from evil.

3. Cats are really fond of this goddess.

4. This god is a bit of a snappy character!

1.Anubis 2. Horus 3.Bastet 4. Sobek

53 Wooden-built trading ships were propelled by a combination of sail and oar power. Wide-bodied cargo boats were used to ferry cattle across the Nile. The animals stood on deck during the crossing.

Who's who in Ancient Egypt

54 The people of ancient Egypt were organized into three classes: upper, middle and lower. The royal family, government officials, senior priests and priestesses, scribes and doctors made up the upper class. Traders, merchants and craftworkers were middle class. The biggest group of people by far – the unskilled workers – made up the lower class.

◀ The arrangement of Egyptian society can be shown as a pyramid shape. The pharaoh sits at the top of the pyramid, with the huge mass of unskilled labourers at the bottom.

viziers and priests

scribes and noblemen

craftworkers and dancers

carrying grain from the fields

peasant workers winnowing grain

55 The man was the head of any Egyptian household. On his father's death, the eldest son inherited the family's land and riches. Egyptian women had rights and privileges too. They could own property and carry out businesses deals, and women from wealthy families could become doctors or priestesses.

Egypt, Old Kingdom

Egypt, Middle Kingdom

Egypt, New Kingdom

▲ These maps show the extent of the Egyptian empire in the three kingdoms.

56 Most ancient Egyptians lived along the banks of the river Nile or in the river valley. As Egypt became more powerful they spread out, up along the river Nile and around the Mediterranean Sea. Others lived by oases, pools of water in the desert.

57

Rich families had several servants, who worked as maids, cooks and gardeners. In large houses the servants had their own quarters separate from those of the family.

▲ Family life played an important role in ancient Egypt. Couples could adopt children if they were unable to have their own.

58

Dogs and cats were the main family pets. Egyptians also kept pet monkeys and sometimes flocks of tame doves. Some people trained their pet baboons to climb fig trees and pick the ripe fruits.

59

Young children played with wooden and clay toys. Popular toys were carved animals – often with moving parts – spinning tops, toy horses, dolls and clay balls. Children also played games which are still played today, such as leapfrog and tug-o'-war.

I DON'T BELIEVE IT!

Wealthy Egyptians wanted servants in the afterlife too. They were buried with models of servants, called shabtis, that were meant to come to life and look after their dead owner!

Home sweet home

60 Egyptian houses were made from mud bricks dried in the sun. Mud was taken from the river Nile, and straw and pebbles were added to make it stronger. The trunks of palm trees supported the flat roofs. The inside walls of houses were covered with plaster, and often painted. Wealthy Egyptians lived in large houses with several storeys. A poorer family, though, might live in a crowded single room.

◀ A mixture of mud, straw and stones was poured into wooden frames or shaped into bricks and left to harden in the sun.

61 In most Egyptian homes there was a small shrine. Here, members of the family worshipped their household god.

The dwarf god, Bes, was the ancient Egyptian god of children and the home.

62 Egyptians furnished their homes with wooden stools, chairs, tables, storage chests and carved beds. A low three- or four-legged footstool was one of the most popular items of furniture. Mats of woven reeds covered the floors.

63 Rich families lived in spacious villas in the countryside. A typical villa had a pond filled with fish, a walled garden and an orchard of fruit trees.

The Egyptians used woven papyrus mats instead of carpets.

64 **They cooked their food in a clay oven or over an open fire.** Most kitchens were equipped with a cylinder-shaped oven made from bricks of baked clay. They burned either charcoal or wood as fuel. They cooked food in two-handled pottery saucepans.

QUIZ 3

1. Why did the Egyptians bury a boat next to their pharaoh?

2. Which part of the body was left inside a mummy?

3. Who was Howard Carter?

4. Why did farmworkers have nothing to do between July and November each year?

1. So he can use it in the next life 2. The heart 3. The man who discovered the tomb of Tutankhamun 4. The river Nile had flooded the farmland

Senet was a popular board game in ancient Egypt. Experts today think it was probably a bit like ludo.

65 **Pottery lamps provided the lighting in Egyptian homes.** They filled the container with oil and burned a wick made of cotton or flax. Houses had very small windows, and sometimes none at all, so there was often very little natural light. Small windows kept out the strong sunlight, helping to keep houses cool.

66 **In Egypt it was good to eat with your fingers!** In rich households, servants would even bring jugs of water between courses so that people could rinse their hands.

Dressing up

67 Egyptians wore lucky charms called amulets. The charms were meant to protect the wearer from evil spirits and to bring good luck. One of the most popular ones was the wadjat eye of the god Horus. Children wore amulets shaped like fish to protect them from drowning in the river Nile.

◀ The eye of Horus was thought to protect everything behind it. The god Horus had his eye torn out while defending the throne of Egypt. Later, the eye was magically repaired.

▲ winged scarab amulet

◀ fish amulet

68 In Egypt, men and women both wore eye make-up. A special black eye make-up, called kohl, was made from ground-up raw metals mixed with oil. The Egyptians believed it had magical healing powers and could restore bad eyesight and fight eye infections. Egyptians also used face rouge for the cheeks and lips, face powder, paint for fingernails and hair dyes.

wig and box

make-up box

69

Most clothes were made from light-coloured linen. Women wore long dresses, often with pleated cloaks. Noblewomen's dresses were made of the best cloth with beads sewn onto it. Men wore either robes or kilt-like skirts, a piece of linen wrapped around the waist and tied in a decorative knot.

▶ This fine long dress is worn with a see-through cloak. Clothes like these made sure that the people of Egypt kept cool in the hot weather.

70

Wealthy people wore wigs made from human hair or sheep's wool which they kept in special boxes on stands at home. Girls wore their hair in pigtails, while boys mostly had shaved heads, sometimes with a plaited lock on one side.

wigs

comb

hair pins

comb

▲ Wigs were often long and elaborate and needed a lot of attention. Egyptians cared for their wigs with combs made of wood and ivory. They sometimes used curling tongs as well.

MAKE A MAGIC EYE CHARM

You will need

self-hardening modelling clay
a length of leather strip or thick cord
a pencil   poster paints
a paintbrush   varnish

Knead the clay until soft and then shape into a wadjat eye. Add extra clay for the pupil of the eye and at the top of the charm. Use the pencil to make the top piece into a loop.

Leave the clay to harden. Paint in bright colours and leave to dry. Varnish. Thread the leather strip or cord through the loop and wear your charm for extra luck.

71

Sandals were made from papyrus and other reeds. Rich people, courtiers and kings and queens wore padded leather ones. Footwear was a luxury item, and most ordinary people walked around barefoot. Colourful pictures of sandals were even painted onto the feet of mummies!

▼ leather sandals

▼ reed sandals

Baking and brewing

72 Bread was the most important food in the diet of ancient Egypt. Harvested grain was stored in huge granaries until needed. The Egyptians' favourite drink was beer. It was very thick and had to be strained before drinking. Models of brewers were even left in tombs to make sure the dead person had a plentiful supply of beer in the next world!

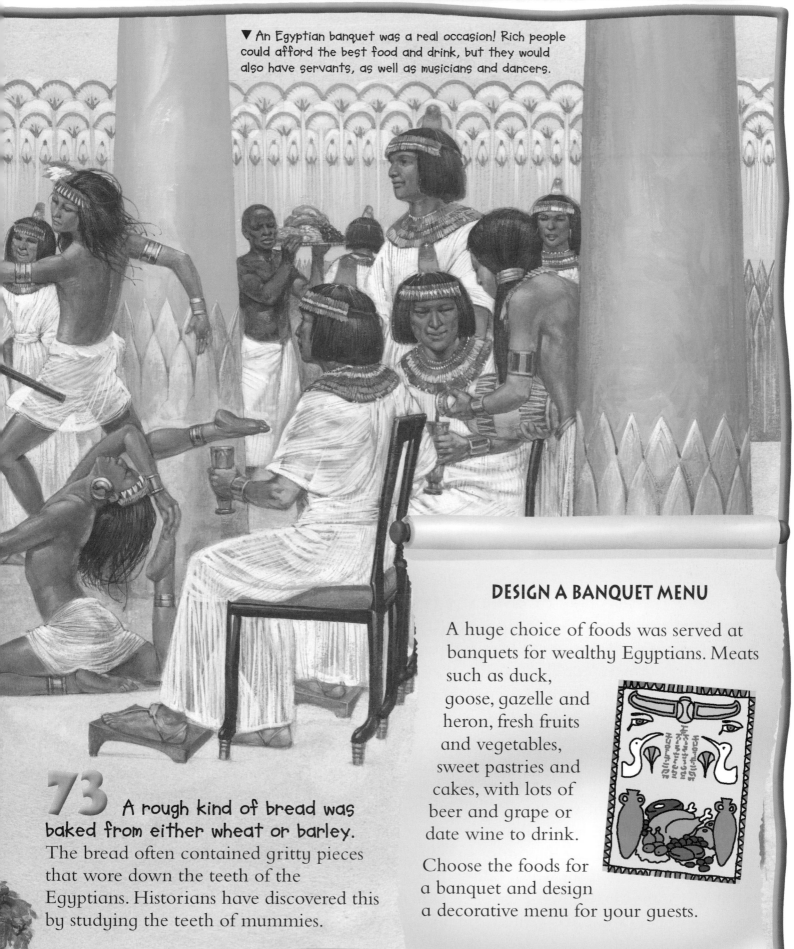

▼ An Egyptian banquet was a real occasion! Rich people could afford the best food and drink, but they would also have servants, as well as musicians and dancers.

DESIGN A BANQUET MENU

A huge choice of foods was served at banquets for wealthy Egyptians. Meats such as duck, goose, gazelle and heron, fresh fruits and vegetables, sweet pastries and cakes, with lots of beer and grape or date wine to drink.

Choose the foods for a banquet and design a decorative menu for your guests.

73 A rough kind of bread was baked from either wheat or barley. The bread often contained gritty pieces that wore down the teeth of the Egyptians. Historians have discovered this by studying the teeth of mummies.

Hard day's work

74 Scribes were very important people in ancient Egypt. These highly skilled men kept records of everything that happened from day to day. They recorded all the materials used for building work, the numbers of cattle, and the crops that had been gathered for the royal family, the government and the temples.

◄ Only the sons of scribes could undergo the strict scribe training, which began as early as the age of nine.

75 The libraries of ancient Egypt held thousands of papyrus scrolls. They covered subjects such as astronomy, medicine, geography and law. Most ordinary Egyptians could not read or write, so the libraries were used only by educated people such as scribes and doctors.

76 Imagine if there were 700 letters in the alphabet! That was how many hieroglyphs Egyptian schoolchildren had to learn! Hieroglyphs were symbols that the Egyptians used for writing. Some symbols stood for words and some for sounds. Children went to schools for scribes where they first learned how to read and write hieroglyphs.

▼ Craftworkers produced statues and furniture for the pharoah. Workers such as these often had their own areas within a town. The village of Deir el–Medina was built specially for those who worked on tombs in the Valley of the Kings.

77 Most people worked as craftworkers or farm labourers. Craftworkers included carpenters, potters, weavers, jewellers, shoemakers, glassblowers and perfume makers. Many sold their goods from small shops in the towns. They were kept busy making items for the pharaoh and wealthy people.

78 A typical lunch for a worker consisted of bread and onions. They may also have had a cucumber, washed down with a drink of beer.

QUIZ 4

Can you name the following items from life in ancient Egypt?

1.

2.

3.

4.

1.The dwarf god Bes 2.A canopic jar 3.A hair comb 4.An amulet

79 The base of the Great Pyramid takes up almost as much space as five football pitches! Huge quantities of stone were needed to build these monuments. The Egyptians quarried limestone, sandstone and granite for their buildings. In the surrounding desert they mined gold for decorations.

80 Slaves were often prisoners who had been captured from Egypt's enemies. They also came from the neighbouring countries of Kush and Nubia. Life as a slave was not all bad. A slave could own land and buy goods – he could even buy his freedom!

Clever Egyptians

81 The insides of many Egyptian tombs were decorated with brightly coloured wall paintings. They often depicted scenes from the dead person's life, showing him or her as a healthy young person. The Egyptians believed that these scenes would come to life in the next world.

sunken relief

raised relief

▶ The Egyptians produced raised reliefs by cutting away the background, and sunken relief by cutting stone from inside the outline.

82 Egyptian sculptors carved enormous stone statues of their pharaohs and gods. These were often placed outside a tomb or temple to guard the entrance. Scenes, called reliefs, were carved into the walls of temples and tombs. These often showed the person as they were when they were young, enjoying scenes from daily life. This was so that when the god Osiris brought the dead person and the tomb paintings back to life, the tomb owners would have a good time in the afterlife!

83 The ancient Egyptians had three different calendars: an everyday farming one, an astronomical and a lunar (Moon) calendar. The 365-day farming calendar was made up of three seasons of four months. The astronomical calendar was based on observations of the star Sirius, which reappeared each year at the start of the flood season. Priests kept a calendar based on the movements of the Moon which told them when to perform ceremonies for to the moon god Khonsu.

▲ The days on this calendar are written in black and red. Black days are ordinary, but the red days are unlucky.

◄ Several artists worked on the tomb paintings. A junior artist drew the outlines of the scene, which were then checked and corrected by a more senior artist. Next, painters filled in the outlines in colour.

84 Astronomers recorded their observations of the night skies. The Egyptian calendar was based on the movement of Sirius, the brightest star in the sky. The Egyptians used their knowledge of astronomy to build temples which lined up with certain stars or with the movement of the Sun.

I DON'T BELIEVE IT!
Bulbs of garlic were used to ward off snakes and to get rid of tapeworms from people's bodies.

85 Egyptian doctors knew how to set broken bones and treat illnesses such as fevers. They used medicines made from plants such as garlic and juniper to treat sick people. The Egyptians had a good knowledge of the basic workings of the human body.

86 The Egyptians used a device called a nilometer to measure the depth of the river Nile. They inserted measuring posts into the riverbed at intervals along the bank so they could check the water levels at the start of each flood season.

From pictures to words

87 **The Egyptians had no paper – they wrote on papyrus.** It was made from the tall papyrus reeds that grew on the banks of the Nile. At first papyrus was sold as long strips, or scrolls, tied with string. Later the Egyptians put the papyrus sheets into books. Papyrus is very long lasting; sheets of papyrus have survived 3,000 years to the present day.

88 **Ink was made by mixing water with soot, charcoal or coloured minerals.** Scribes wrote in ink on papyrus scrolls, using reed brushes with specially shaped ends.

1. Papyrus was expensive because it took a long time to make. First people had to cut down the papyrus stems, and cut them up into lots of thin strips.

2. Then someone laid these strips in rows on a frame to form layers.

3. The papyrus strips were then pressed under weights. This squeezed out the water and squashed the layers together.

4. Finally, when the papyrus was dry, a man with a stone rubbed the surface smooth for writing.

89

The Rosetta Stone was found in 1799 by a French soldier in Egypt. It is a large slab of stone onto which three different kinds of writing have been carved: hieroglyphics, a simpler form of hieroglyphics called demotic and Greek. All three sets of writing give an account of the coronation of King Ptolemy V. By translating the Greek, scholars could understand the Egyptian writing for the first time.

90

The ancient Egyptians used a system of picture writing called hieroglyphics. Each hieroglyph represented an object or a sound. For example, the picture of a lion represented the sound 'l'; a basket represented the word 'lord'. Altogether there were about 700 different hieroglyphs. Scribes wrote them on papyrus scrolls or carved them into stone.

91

In the 5th century BC a Greek historian called Herodotus wrote about life in ancient Egypt. As he travelled across the country he observed and wrote about people's daily lives, and their religion and customs such as embalming and mummification – he even wrote about cats!

WRITE YOUR NAME IN HIEROGLYPHICS

Below you will see the hieroglyphic alphabet. I have written my name in hieroglyphs. Can you write yours?

J A N E

A B C D E F G H
I J K L M N O P
Q R S T U V W X Y Z

92

The hieroglyphs of a ruler's name were written inside an oval-shaped frame called a cartouche. The pharaoh's cartouche was carved on pillars and temple walls, painted on tomb walls and mummy cases and written on official documents.

Fun and games

93 Hippo hunting was a dangerous but popular sport in ancient Egypt. Hunters in reed boats, armed only with spears and ropes, killed hippos in the waters of the Nile. In the desert, hunters chased lions, antelope, wild bulls, gazelles and hares. Marsh birds were killed with throwing sticks that were like boomerangs.

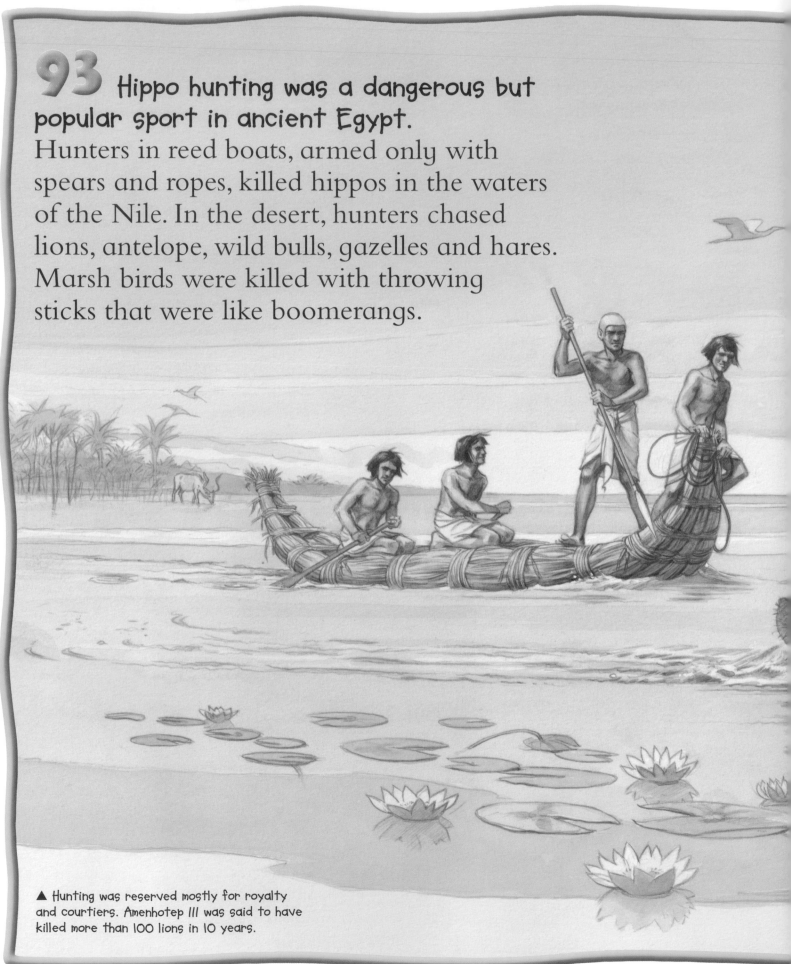

▲ Hunting was reserved mostly for royalty and courtiers. Amenhotep III was said to have killed more than 100 lions in 10 years.

MAKE A SNAKE GAME
You will need

a sheet of thick cardboard
a large dinner plate   a paintbrush
scissors   coloured pens
white paint   counters
a pencil   two dice

Place the plate on the card and draw round the outside. Cut out the circle. Paint one side with paint. Leave to dry.

Draw a snake's head in the centre of the board. Draw small circles (about 2 cm across) spreading out from the centre until you reach the edge of the board. Colour the circles to make an attractive pattern.

Place a counter for each player on the outside square. The winner is the first player to reach the snake's head.

94 The Egyptians played various board games, a few of which we still play today. The game of senet was supposed to represent the struggle between good and evil on the journey into the next world. Players moved sets of counters across the board according to how their throwing sticks (like modern dice) landed. Another popular board game was called hounds and jackals.

Heroes and heroines

95 **Ramses II built more temples than any other Egyptian ruler.** Two of his greatest achievements are the huge rock-cut temple at Abu Simbel and the Great Hall at Karnak. He also finished building the mortuary temple of Seti I at Luxor. After his death a further nine pharaohs were given the name Ramses.

Lapis lazuli is a bright-blue semi-precious gem that the Egyptians used to decorate the coffins of rich people.

▼ The Great Hall at Karnak

96 **Queen Hatshepsut was often depicted wearing men's clothing and a false beard.** She was the wife of Thutmose II. On his death Hatshepsut took the title of pharaoh and adopted the royal symbols of the double crown, the crook, the flail (whip) – and also the ceremonial beard!

▶ During her 20-year reign Hatshepsut sent an expedition of five ships to Punt on the coast of the Red Sea. The ships brought back incense, copper and ivory.

Mark Antony   Cleopatra

97 **Queen Cleopatra VII was one of the last rulers of ancient Egypt.** She fell in love with the Roman emperor Julius Caesar, and later married the Roman general Mark Antony. Cleopatra killed herself in 30 BC when the Romans conquered Egypt.

◀ The pharaoh Tutankhamun was buried in three separate coffins. Each coffin was specially made to go around the one inside. This is the middle coffin. Like all the coffins, it is made of gold, but this one is also inlaid with a gem called lapis lazuli.

Narmer pulette

100 King Menes was the first ruler of a united Egypt. He joined together the kingdoms of Upper and Lower Egypt, under one government, in around 3100 BC. Menes was also called Narmer. Archaeologists have found a slate tablet, called the Narmer Palette, that shows him beating his enemies in battle.

98 Tutankhamun is probably the most famous pharaoh of all. His tomb, with its fabulous treasure of over 5,000 objects, was discovered complete in 1922. Tutankhamun was only nine years old when he became ruler, and he died at the young age of about 17. He was buried in the Valley of the Kings.

99 Thutmose III was a clever general who added new lands to ancient Egypt. Under his leadership, Egypt's armies seized territory in Syria to the north and Palestine to the east. During his reign Thutmose ordered a giant obelisk made of granite to be placed at Heliopolis – it now stands on the bank of the river Thames in London.

QUIZ 5

1. Name two popular drinks in ancient Egypt.

2. What is a cartouche?

3. What is the Rosetta Stone?

4. What is senet?

5. Explain why Queen Hatshepsut was unusual.

1. Beer and wine 2. An oval plaque on which the pharaoh's name was written. 3. The stone that enabled historians to read hieroglyphs. 4. An ancient Egyptian game. 5. She ruled as a pharaoh, wearing the ceremonial beard.

Index

A

Abu Simbel **17**, 28, 46
afterlife 31, 40
Alexandria **23**, 28
altar/shrine 32
Amenhotep/Akhenaten **15**
amulets 34
astronomers 41

B

barter 24
beer 36
boats and ships **23**, **28**, **29**, 44
bread 36, 37

C

calendars **40**
canopic jars 20
Carnarvon, Lord **16**
Carter, Howard **17**
cartouche 43
chariots **22**
Cleopatra VII, Queen **46**
clothes **35**
cooking and eating 33
craftworkers **38**, **39**
crops 6, 26, 27
crown, double **11**

D E F

deben 25
doctors **41**
dynasties 10
embalming 15
families **30**, 31, 32
farmers 6, 11, **26–27**
food **26**, **36–37**, 39

G

gods and goddesses 14–15, 17
    Amun-Ra 17
    Anubis **15**
    Aten 15
    Bastet **14**
    Bes **32**
    Horus **15**, 34
    Isis **15**
    Osiris **15**, 40
    Ra **14**
    Sobek **14**
    Thoth **14**
gold mines 24, 39
grain 27, 36
Great Pyramid, Giza **12–13**, 18–19, 39
Great Sphinx, Giza **13**

H I

hair cones 9
Hatshepsut, Queen **46**
Herodotus 43
hieroglyphs 14, 38, **42**, **43**
history 10–11
houses 32, 33
hunting **44**
Hyksos 22, 23
Imhotep 19
ink **43**
irrigation 26

K L

Karnak 28, **46**
Kerma 24, 28
Khufu, King 12
    funerary boat 12, 29
lamps **33**
Lower Egypt (Nile Delta) 11, 47

M

make-up **34**
market **24–25**
mask, death **16**, 20
Menes, King 47
Middle Kingdom 10, 30
mud bricks 32
mummies, making 15, **20–21**
mummy cases/coffins 17, **21**, 47

N O

Narmer Palette **47**
New Kingdom 10, 30
Nile **6**, 28, 30
    floods 6, 26
    nilometer **41**
obelisk **47**
Old Kingdom 10, 30

P

papyrus 28, 38, **42**, 44
people, classes of **30**
Pepi II **10**
pets 20, 31
pharaohs **8–9**
Pharos 23
priests 17
Ptolemy 23
Punt 25, 46
pyramids **12–13**, **18–19**

R

Ramses II **9**, 17, 46
Ramses III 23
reliefs **40**
Rosetta Stone **43**

S

sandals **35**
sarcophagus 17, 21
scarab amulet **34**
schoolchildren 38
scribes **38**, 42, 43
Sea People 23
senet 45
servants 31
shabtis 31
shaduf **26**
slaves 24, 39
soldiers **22**
statues 40
Step Pyramid, Saqqara **12**, 19
stone blocks 18, 19, 29

T

temples 17, 46
Thutmose III 47
tomb robbers 13, **16**
tombs 16–17, 40
toys 31
trade 24, 25
Tutankhamun **16**, 17, 47

U V W

underworld 15
Upper Egypt (Nile Valley) 11, 47
Valley of the Kings 16, 28
viziers **11**
wadjat eye **34**
wall paintings 40, 41
weapons 22
wigs **35**